The Urbana Free Library

Humvees
High Mobility in the Field

Michael Teitelbaum

Enslow Publishers, Inc.
40 Industrial Road
Box 398
Berkeley Heights, NJ 07922
USA

http://www.enslow.com

1-07

Library of Congress Cataloging-in-Publication Data

Teitelbaum, Michael.
 Humvees : high mobility in the field / by Michael Teitelbaum.
    p. cm. — (Mighty military machines)
 Includes bibliographical references and index.
 ISBN 0-7660-2661-2
 1. Hummer trucks—Juvenile literature. 2. United States—Armed Forces—Transportation—Juvenile literature. I. Title. II. Series.

 UG618.T46 2006
 623.7'4722—dc22

                                    2005037384

Printed in the United States of America

10 9 8 7 6 5 4 3 2 1

To Our Readers:
We have done our best to make sure all Internet Addresses in this book were active and appropriate when we went to press. However, the author and the publisher have no control over and assume no liability for the material available on those Internet sites or on other Web sites they may link to. Any comments or suggestions can be sent by e-mail to comments@enslow.com or to the address on the back cover.

Photo Credits: Courtesy of AM General, pp. 3, 25, 39; Associated Press, AP, pp. 4, 44; Associated Press/Daily Press, p. 43; Associated Press/Kentucky Army National Guard, p. 28; Associated Press/Roswell Daily Record, pp. 1, 17; CORBIS/Leif Skoogfors, p. 27; CORBIS/Peter Turnley, p. 9; Department of Defense, pp. 3, 10, 14, 16 (both), 20, 22, 30 (top), 33, 34, 38, 40, 46, 47; FEMA, p. 45; Getty Images, pp. 36-37; Getty Images/Joe Raedle, p. 12; Getty Images/Robert Nickelsberg, p. 30 (bottom); Getty Images/Stan Honda, AFP, p. 41; Library of Congress, p. 19; XNR Productions, p. 7.

Cover Photos: Getty Images/Scott Nelson, front; Department of Defense, back.

Contents

Chapter ONE

Observe and Identify

A Humvee rolled slowly through a dark jungle in Panama. Hidden in the back of the vehicle was a four-man team of Marines working in secret. They were to slip into a location, do their job, then slip back out, without anyone ever knowing they had been there.

The year was 1989. Deep in this Central American jungle, the U.S. government had a place where thousands of gallons of fuel were stored in large tanks. This fuel was used to run U.S. military vehicles in Panama. The United States feared that terrorists could attack the storage area, igniting and destroying the fuel.

There were many terrorist groups operating in Panama at that time. The U.S. government wanted to know which one was trying to disrupt or destroy the fuel storage area. Guards were posted around the area, but they could not patrol the entire area at all times. That is where secret sensors came in.

These special sensors were hidden throughout the area. They could detect movement. If intruders entered, a signal was sent to Marines posted a short distance away. It was then that the Humvee was sent out.

The four Marines hidden in the back of the Humvee were part of the Marines' special operations forces, known as Reconnaissance, or "Recon" Marines. They were not to confront the intruders. That way, those being watched would have no idea that anyone was watching them.

With the four-man team hidden from sight in the back, the Humvee rolled into action. Once in place, the team's mission was to watch the intruders and, if possible, to identify them. The key to the mission's success was remaining unseen.

The Mission

For this mission, the Humvee had a two-man crew: the driver, and a second Marine riding in the passenger seat next to him. This is called "riding shotgun." The Marine in the passenger seat carried an automatic weapon.

The back of the Humvee was set up to carry cargo, such as food or weapons. But the "cargo" it carried this night was the four-man Marine special operations team. They hid in the cargo area under a canvas tarp, which was normally used to protect cargo from the rain. The Marines were operating as spies. And if they were caught, their entire mission, as well as their lives, would be in danger.

The operation was a special mission, but it used an everyday mission as its cover. At that time, Humvees were being used regularly in the Panamanian jungles for Psychological Operations. These special missions were known as "PSYOPS" for short. PSYOPS were used to keep the opposing side nervous and unable to predict what would happen

PSYOPS were used to keep the opposing side nervous and unable to predict what would happen next.

next. Some PSYOPS were also used to keep the opposing side awake for long periods of time. This made them less efficient during a battle.

The PSYOPS worked liked this: Humvees drove through the jungle, both day and night. As they went, they blasted hard-rock music from two enormous loudspeakers mounted to the top of the Humvee. The huge speakers were five feet wide

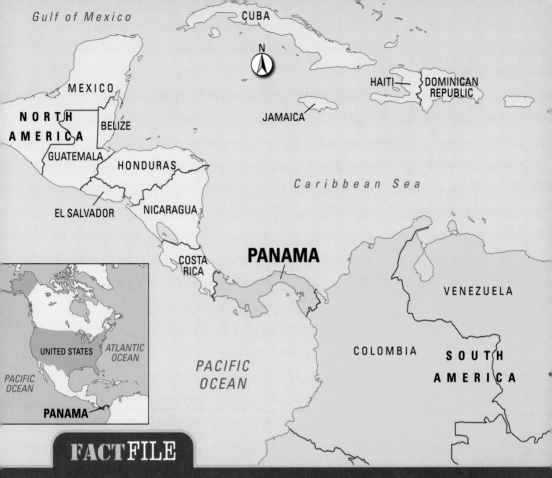

FACTFILE

Facts About the U.S. Invasion of Panama

• The purpose of the invasion was to capture Panamanian leader Manuel Noriega, and to establish a democratic government in Panama. Noriega was accused of sending drugs to be sold in the United States.

• In December 1989, Noriega declared a state of war with the United States. A day later, an unarmed U.S. Marine was killed by Noriega's forces. Shortly after, the United States sent troops to Panama and began bombing targets throughout the country.

• Noriega was captured in January 1990 and sentenced to forty years in a U.S. federal prison for drug trafficking. Although Noriega was removed from power, Panama still struggles to establish a solid democracy.

and played extremely loudly. For this operation, the music chosen was the song "Welcome to the Jungle," by Guns N' Roses.

On the night of the special mission, the usual two-man Humvee crew of the driver and the Marine riding shotgun drove slowly through the jungle blasting the music, as the Recon Marines crouched silently in the back. This provided perfect cover for their covert operation.

With the Humvee still moving, the four Marines swiftly leaped from the vehicle. Hitting the ground and staying low, they slipped into the darkness of the jungle. The Humvee drove off into the night.

Dressed to blend in with the thick trees and plants, the Marines moved like jungle cats, focused on their destination—the fuel storage facility. When they reached the building, they shimmied up tall trees. Hiding near the treetops, they had a clear view of the facility below.

Their mission was simple, but dangerous. While staying perfectly silent, the Marines had to keep watch. They had to note the appearance and actions of the trespassers. How many were there? What kind of weapons did they carry? Which terrorist group did they belong to? They had to be sure the terrorists would not spot them. A rustle of leaves or a cough or sneeze at the wrong moment could give their position away. Then they would be easy targets for the weapons of the

FACTFILE

Camouflage

Humvees are very versatile. This means that they can be used for many purposes by many branches of the armed forces. They are also versatile in the way they look. Humvees can be painted to blend into their environment. This makes it harder for the opposing side to spot them. Sand-colored paint makes Humvees harder to spot while moving through the desert. For jungle missions, like the one in Panama, green, brown, and black camouflage paint helps a Humvee blend in.

FACTFILE

Night Vision

Humvees can carry many weapons and pieces of equipment. One of the most important is a night vision viewer. This allows soldiers on a Humvee to do surveillance, or spy, after dark. Night vision viewers and goggles work by collecting and boosting the tiny amounts of light that are still available at night.

The lens of the night vision viewer collects extremely tiny particles of moonlight or starlight. Then discs inside the viewer change and magnify the light particles to thousands of times their original size. The particles next strike a green phosphor screen, which glows brightly with the image of the night scene in the viewer.

terrorists. To survive, the Marines had to use their skills to stay perfectly silent and still.

After a while, their eyes adjusted to the dark. Some of them used night vision goggles to get a clearer look at the ground below.

Suddenly the sound of people walking through the jungle cut through the night. The intruders were near. The Marines carefully noted the number of terrorists. Trained to recognize the uniforms of various terrorist groups, the Marines recorded those details. The terrorists' automatic weapons, fully loaded and slung across their shoulders, were also noted.

The intruders were on their own spying mission tonight. Once they saw what they came to see, they slipped back into the jungle. They did not know that they had been watched. The trees had eyes and ears, in the form of four highly-trained Marines.

To survive, the Marines had to use their skills to stay perfectly silent and still.

Just before sunrise, the four Marines scrambled back down the trees to another Humvee, also blasting music. The Marines dove into the back of the moving Humvee and covered themselves with the tarp.

The Humvee finished its normal PSYOPS route and returned the Marines to their base. There, once again out of harm's way, the Marines reported their findings to their superior officers. They had gotten good information that night about the terrorist group that might attack the fuel storage area. This knowledge helped prevent that attack. It was also later used to help plan a U.S.-led invasion of Panama.

Chapter TWO

What Is a Humvee?

The word "Humvee" is taken from the abbreviation for the real name of the vehicle. The <u>Hi</u>gh <u>M</u>obility <u>M</u>ulti-purpose <u>W</u>heeled <u>V</u>ehicle (HMMWV) is called a "Jeep on steroids" by the soldiers who use it.

The Humvee is one vehicle that can do many jobs. It replaced a number of other military vehicles that could do only one job each. The work of lighter jeeps, heavier all-terrain cargo carriers, and Army ambulances were all taken over by the more versatile Humvee in 1985.

Although Humvees are large, they are lighter than some of the vehicles they replaced. Humvees are also easier to take care of, more reliable, and stand up better to heavy-duty use over time.

Humvees are very mobile. This means that they move easily over many different surfaces. Four-wheel drive helps Humvees operate everywhere from sandy deserts to rain-soaked jungles, and from steep mountains to bumpy, unpaved roads. They can even drive across the bottom of a five-foot-deep river without floating away.

Humvees can travel hundreds of miles, with only small amounts of maintenance. Humvees must often carry their cargo and passengers safely while dodging bullets, bombs, and mines (explosives hidden in the ground).

Humvees operate everywhere from sandy deserts to rain-soaked jungles.

Humvees are tough. Their bodies are made of aluminum, a metal that does not rust. The body and its special shock absorbers are designed to bend and give on bumpy, rutted, or rocky terrain, where other vehicles might crack or come apart. This gives the Humvee a longer life.

Humvees also have special tires called "runflat" tires. Even if they are punctured, they allow the vehicle to keep moving. These tires have very thick walls that can support the tires even if they lose air pressure. The driver does not have to stop, get out, and fix or change the tire. This is especially important in combat situations.

In some Humvees, the driver can change the tire pressure right from the driver's seat. This allows the vehicle to adapt to changing terrain. The Humvee has power steering which makes it easier to turn the steering wheel. Because of this, Humvees are easier to drive than the old jeeps and trucks they replaced. A Humvee moves slowly and steadily over rough terrain. However, it can reach speeds of

over seventy miles per hour on paved roads. It also has high ground clearance, which means that its body sits very high off the ground. This allows the Humvee to travel over rocky, snowy, or densely overgrown terrain.

But the Humvee's most important feature is its versatility, the ability to change and do many things.

What Else Can Humvees Do?

The Humvee's design allows it to be changed for many different uses. No matter what the Humvee is doing, though, its engine, chassis (body), and transmission (the system that moves the vehicle) stay the same. Many of its other parts can be changed depending on the Humvee's mission.

One use for a Humvee is to transport troops. For this purpose, extra benches are added in the cargo area. Humvees are also used to carry shipments of cargo, like food or medical supplies. Sometimes they carry shipments of weapons and ammunition. In this case, the cargo area is left open with no seats. At other times, the Humvee is fitted with powerful weapons of its own, like machine guns or anti-tank missile launchers. Then the Humvee becomes a combat vehicle.

◄ This Humvee is equipped with four separate tracks to help it move easily through the snow. It was being tested at a training area in California.

What Goes on a Humvee?

Machine Gun

One of the main weapons that can be attached to a Humvee when it is being used as a combat vehicle is a machine gun. Machine guns can fire many bullets very quickly. A Humvee's machine gun is mounted on a turret. The turret allows the gun to rotate in a complete circle so that its operator can fire bullets in any direction.

Night Vision Viewer

This special piece of equipment is used for nighttime surveillance (spying) missions. With it, soldiers are able to see more in the dark.

Anti-tank Missile Launchers

These tubes are mounted on the roof of a Humvee. They are used to launch missiles, which are powerful explosive weapons that can destroy tanks or other large vehicles.

Anti-tank Missile Launchers

Winch

A winch is a machine used to tow vehicles or equipment or to pull them out of ditches. It includes a spool of thick cable with a hook on the end and a powerful motor, which rolls up the cable after it is attached to whatever vehicle it is trying to help.

Loudspeakers

Five-foot-wide loudspeakers can be attached to the roof of a Humvee for blasting loud music. These are used for psychological operations (PSYOPS).

With a special attachment called a winch, which mounts at the front of the Humvee frame, the Humvee can be used to tow other vehicles or to rescue vehicles that have gotten stuck or have flipped over. The winch's cable, motor, and hook can pull other vehicles out of ditches.

Finally, Humvees can be used as ambulances in combat zones. When set up as an ambulance, the Humvee can carry either four wounded soldiers on stretchers or eight wounded soldiers sitting on the built-in bench seats along each side of the rear compartment.

Humvees can transport people, cargo, and weapons. They can tow and rescue other vehicles. They can function as combat vehicles fitted with weapons, or can help save lives as ambulances. Humvees are easy to operate and take care of. They can do all of these things in a variety of places, from open deserts to dense jungles and raging rivers.

How Humvees Came to Be

In 1979, the U.S. Army decided that it wanted a new vehicle. It was looking for something that could replace several existing vehicles with one versatile new machine. The Army jeep, the all-terrain cargo vehicle known as the "Mule," and the Army ambulance had all been in use for many years. In fact, many of these vehicles still in service at that time were twenty years old. And, having three different vehicles meant that soldiers who operated and took care of them had to learn all about the three different machines.

The Army was ready for a vehicle that could serve as a combat machine equipped with weapons and also act as a combat-support vehicle, carrying troops, supplies, and medical equipment. They

▼ The Army jeep was used for decades. It was one of the vehicles replaced by the much larger, sturdier, and more useful Humvee. This jeep was photographed in 1943.

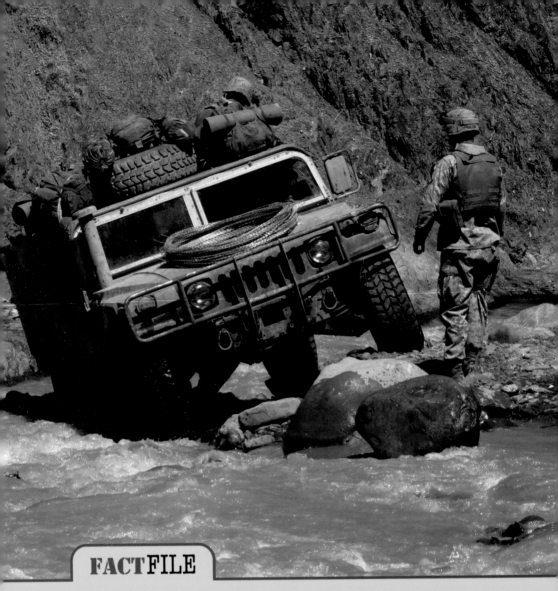

FACTFILE

The Proving Ground

Before delivering it to the Army, AM General tested the Humvee for more than six hundred thousand miles. The company took its new vehicle over rugged courses that imitated off-road conditions around the world in combat environments. Humvees were driven over rocky hills, through deep sand and mud, in water up to sixty inches (five feet) deep, in desert heat over one hundred degrees, and in Arctic cold at temperatures of twenty below zero.

wanted a versatile machine that could operate in a number of very different environments.

They also wanted a vehicle that was safer and performed better. They wanted a vehicle that was faster, lightweight, and better able to move cross-country quickly.

Three companies bid on the project and submitted designs. In 1983, AM General was awarded the contract and started building the High Mobility Multi-purpose Wheeled Vehicle (HMMWV, which came to be pronounced "Humvee").

Although the Humvee answered many of the Army's needs for a new vehicle, it is not perfect. Its main weakness is that its basic lightweight body is very vulnerable to attacks by Improvised Explosive Devices (IEDs). These are homemade bombs often used in roadside attacks.

IEDs can be hidden in everyday objects like plastic bags, orange crates, or rusted gasoline cans. Soldiers driving Humvees cannot tell them apart from normal roadside garbage. Some IEDs have even been stuffed into the bodies of dead animals. IEDs are also triggered by remote control, so the bomber can be hidden when the bomb goes off. The Army is working on reinforcing the Humvee's armor to make it safer against IEDs.

The Army is working on reinforcing the Humvee to make it safer against IEDs.

Chapter THREE

Bouncing Over Rough Roads

Army Private First Class (PFC) James Toole placed the huge cooler into the back of his Humvee. Then he loaded the cooler with eggs, fruit, milk, and meat. He knew the difficult, fourteen-hour operation ahead was not exactly a typical heroic mission by Hollywood's standards, but that did not make it any less important—or any less dangerous.

It was 1993 and PFC Toole was in the former Republic of Macedonia on the border of Serbia, in Eastern Europe. He was there as part of a United Nations (U.N.) Protection Force. U.S. Army troops patrolled the border. Toole's mission was to bring much-needed food to the troops stationed along this dangerous border.

Although Humvees saw their share of military combat, the all-purpose vehicle often proved its worth as a simple supply carrier. The mission in Macedonia was no exception.

PFC Toole drove the Humvee over the rutted, narrow mountain roads. The supplies had to get through or the troops along the border would be stranded with nothing to eat in an area filled with opposing soldiers.

Joining Toole on this mission was Staff Sergeant Johnny Castillo. Castillo rode shotgun, tightly clutching his automatic weapon. Attacks by warring troops were common on these supply runs.

The Mission

The Humvee was the best vehicle to deliver the supplies because it could handle the almost impassable mountain roads. As it climbed the narrow, steep, winding mountain road, it began to rain. The rain grew steadily heavier as the Humvee next descended into a valley on the other side of the mountain. A wide river cut through the valley. As the rain continued to fall and the Humvee rolled slowly along the now muddy, slippery road, the river swelled, rising near the edge of its banks.

But despite the bad weather conditions, the mission had to be completed. The Humvee approached the river. Then it continued—right into the swollen river. The Humvee filled with water to increase its weight and to keep it from floating.

The tires gripped the bottom of the raging river. Slowly, the water in the Humvee covered Toole's and Castillo's boots. It was wet and uncomfortable in the Humvee, but they had to get across the river.

Once they had reached the other side, the water drained out of the Humvee and it continued along the bumpy road. Toole and Castillo passed several farms. Rounding a bend, the soldiers found the road blocked. The road was not blocked by troops, but by a large herd of cattle!

The animals plodded down the road, herded by a farmer toward a grazing field. Toole slowed the Humvee to a crawl. He pulled as far to the right as he could without tipping the vehicle into a ditch that dropped sharply from the edge of the road.

The soldiers grew frustrated by the delay of close to an hour, but it was nothing they had not encountered before. Toole was careful not to injure the cattle or the farmer and careful to keep all the Humvee's wheels firmly on the road.

The road wound further into the countryside. The quiet was shattered by a frightening sound— the barking of wild dogs. Attacks by wild dogs were a constant threat in the hills of Macedonia.

Castillo spotted the pack first. About a dozen wild dogs came tearing down the hillside heading right for the Humvee, barking and snarling. Castillo aimed his automatic weapon into the air and fired a few rounds.

The blasts echoed in the mountains. The dogs slowed their run, startled by the loud sound. Castillo did not want to shoot the animals and would do so only if he felt that his life and Toole's life were in immediate danger.

Several of the bolder dogs moved slowly toward the Humvee. It seemed that the noise alone was not going to stop them. Aiming carefully, Castillo pointed his weapon at the ground a few yards in front of the lead dog. Then he fired.

Bullets struck the ground, scattering dirt in all directions. That did it. The dogs turned and ran back up the hill.

Toole remarked that it had been a close call, and Castillo agreed.

The Humvee rolled on. As the two soldiers entered the last village before reaching their destination, they were mobbed by a crowd of curious children. The enormous Humvee fascinated the local children. They ran beside it, touching the doors and fenders. Again, Toole had to drive extremely carefully to avoid injuring any of the children. Crawling through town, they finally cleared the group and picked up speed.

At last, they spotted the first border outpost along the road where U.S. troops were anxiously waiting for the Humvee. Pulling into the outpost, Toole and Castillo had many helping hands unloading the fresh food for their fellow soldiers.

After several more stops along the border, the two soldiers headed back to their base. The return trip was uneventful and this routine mission was completed successfully. Toole and Castillo were proud of the way their Humvee had done its job. The Humvee was truly the only vehicle that could have made it to the outpost and back again safely.

FACTFILE

Just Dropping In!

Sometimes Humvees are parachuted into difficult-to-reach places. The vehicle is strapped to a metal platform, which has large parachutes attached to it. The platform, with the Humvee attached, is then dropped from the back of a cargo plane.

Unlike paratroopers, who can jump from planes or helicopters many thousands of feet in the air, Humvees are dropped from just a few hundred feet above the ground—or closer! While a person can steer a parachute after he or she jumps, a parachuting Humvee cannot be steered. So the shorter the distance it has to fall, the more likely it is to land where it is needed.

Troops then parachute down beside the vehicle, arriving exactly where they need to be, ready to begin their mission.

Chapter FOUR

Quick Thinking, Swift Action

Sergeant Leigh Ann Hester, a National Guard soldier in the Military Police (MP), knew this mission would be dangerous. It was March 20, 2005, and she was in Iraq. Sergeant Hester was team leader of an MP patrol. Her unit was part of the 617th Military Police Company of Richmond, Kentucky. She was driving a Humvee, following a supply convoy, or group of trucks carrying supplies. Beside her in the shotgun seat was Staff Sergeant Timothy Nein.

The mission of the 617th was to travel with the convoy along the busy supply route outside Baghdad,

Iraq's capital city. They were to keep a watchful eye out for attacks from the sides and rear of the convoy. Hester and the eight other members of her company, all in Humvees, were armed and ready. They each had the same mission: to protect the convoy and make sure that the much-needed supplies arrived safely. They hoped not to engage in actual combat. But that hope would soon be shattered.

The Mission

Sergeant Hester's Humvee trailed behind the supply convoy. She knew that in recent months attacks by Iraqi insurgents against U.S. troops had increased. The insurgents are Iraqis opposed to the U.S. military presence in Iraq.

Suddenly, just outside of Baghdad, this routine mission became anything but routine when about a dozen insurgents attacked the convoy. They had been hiding in trenches alongside the road. They fired automatic weapons from the trenches and tossed grenades, or small bombs, at the supply trucks to try and destroy them.

Bullets rained down all around Sergeant Hester. Explosions tore up the road in front of her Humvee. She jammed down on the Humvee's accelerator and pulled the steering wheel hard to

Humvee "Skins"

There are two types of Humvees. Standard or "light-skinned" Humvees are one type. These offer little protection against Improvised Explosive Devices (IEDs), the main threat to Humvees being used in Iraq. These roadside bombs have proved deadly against light-skinned Humvees.

The Army has been refitting these vehicles with armor kits to protect the soldiers operating them. The armor kits contain special panels that bolt onto and protect important parts of the Humvee, like the engine and transmission. The kits also contain armor-hardened doors, seats, and windshields. Special armored plates protect the underside of the vehicle.

The other type of Humvee is built with stronger armor right at the factory. These are called up-armored Humvees (one is shown below).

Before the official refitting kits arrived, soldiers in Iraq put their own armor on their Humvees. They used scrap metal in an attempt to strengthen their vehicles. The issue of armor became controversial, as some people questioned why soldiers were sent into battle without fully armored Humvees.

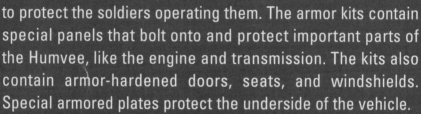

the right. The vehicle took off, gaining speed. Hugging the side of the road, Hester sped past the group of insurgents in the trenches who were firing on the supply trucks. As Hester drove, Staff Sergeant Nein fired his automatic weapon into the trenches.

Gripping the wheel tightly, Hester moved her Humvee in between the convoy of trucks and the attackers. She hoped to cut off their easy escape route. If they tried to leave the trenches to get away, they would have to get past Sergeant Hester.

Hester realized instantly that she had plunged into what soldiers called the "kill zone," the center of intense combat. Her Humvee was now in the thick of the fighting. Screeching to a halt, Hester began firing grenades into the trenches from an M203 grenade launcher.

Then she and Sergeant Nein leaped from the Humvee and entered the trenches, their rifles blazing. In the trenches, Sergeant Hester killed three insurgents with her rifle. The attack on the convoy had been stopped.

When the battle was over, twenty-seven insurgents were dead, six were wounded, and one was captured. Three members of the 617th Military Police Company unit were wounded. But the convoy reached its destination safely thanks to the quick thinking and swift actions of Sergeant Hester.

FACTFILE

Second Generation Humvees

In 1995, a second generation of Humvees was introduced. This new model, called the A2, features a bigger and more powerful engine. The original Humvee had a 6.2-liter engine and could produce 150 horsepower (hp). The A2 has a 6.5-liter engine and generates 160 hp. The A2 also has an improved steering system and is slightly taller and longer than the original. The extra power and improved steering allow A2 drivers to move faster, more easily, and with greater control over rugged terrain.

The Silver Star

On June 16, 2005, Sergeant Leigh Ann Hester, vehicle (Humvee) commander, 617th Military Police Company, Richmond, Kentucky, became the first woman since World War II to be awarded the Silver Star. The Silver Star is a medal awarded for gallantry in action, which means thinking of the safety of others before one's own safety. Hester received the medal at an awards ceremony at Camp Liberty in Iraq.

Sergeant Hester said that she was surprised when she heard that she was being considered for

In June 2005, Humvee driver Sergeant Leigh Ann Hester ▶ became the first woman to receive the Silver Star medal since World War II.

the Silver Star. "I'm honored to even be considered, much less awarded, the medal," she said.

Being the first woman since World War II to receive the medal is important to Hester. But she does not dwell on that fact. "It really doesn't have anything to do with being a female," she said. "It's about the duties I performed that day as a soldier."

Hester has been in the National Guard since April 2001. She said that she did not have time to be scared when the fighting started. She also did not realize the impact of what had happened until much later. "Your training kicks in and the soldier kicks in," she said. "It's your life or theirs. You've got a job to do—protecting yourself and your fellow comrades."

Chapter FIVE

Triangle of Death

Sergeant Joshua Haycox drove his Humvee slowly. He kept a safe distance from the Humvee in front of him. Haycox's vehicle was one of four armored Humvees traveling in a line. This Army convoy was moving into the dangerous area in Iraq south of Baghdad known as the "Triangle of Death." Their mission was to seek out and stop insurgents who had been attacking American troops and Iraqis in Baghdad.

This area was dangerous because, for the most part, it had no government. The area was filled with abandoned farmhouses now taken over by insurgents. It contained old munitions (weapons and ammunition) factories. At one time it had been home to military compounds that housed elite forces of the Iraqi Army under the command of former Iraqi president Saddam Hussein. From there, the insurgents staged attacks on Baghdad.

Haycox and his fellow soldiers knew that they were in extremely dangerous territory.

The Mission

This operation took place in April 2005. Sergeant Haycox's Humvee and the other Humvees in the convoy were carrying troops. All were members of the 3rd Armored Cavalry Regiment. The Humvees had machine guns attached to their rooftop rotating turrets. The soldiers stationed behind the machine guns, called gunners, could fire them in any direction, spinning the weapons in a complete circle. The gunners were ready in case the convoy was attacked.

As Sergeant Haycox drove his Humvee, he scanned the road for roadside bombs. These IEDs had been exploding unexpectedly, damaging Humvees and killing or injuring soldiers all over Iraq. The Triangle of Death was one area where soldiers were likely to encounter IEDs.

The gunner in the turret of Haycox's Humvee stayed low, lifting his head out just far enough to

▲ A Humvee full of soldiers races toward battle in Iraq in 2003. Two soldiers ride on top, ready with a rifle and a machine gun.

see. Suddenly the Humvee just in front of them exploded. It swerved into a ditch, and came to a sudden stop.

Haycox's commander, Colonel H.R. McMaster, ordered him to pull off the road immediately. The colonel was hoping to avoid any more bombs. He ordered the gunner to stand ready. Haycox watched as injured soldiers stumbled out of the bombed

Humvee. Then, he realized that he had been riding in that same Humvee just ten minutes earlier. He could have easily been one of the injured. But there was no time to think about that. Gunfire broke out.

Haycox leaped from the Humvee, firing his rifle.

"Look for the triggerman!" shouted Haycox's gunner from up in the turret. "I can't find the shooter!"

Haycox kept his head down as he raced to help his injured buddies from the bombed Humvee. Colonel McMaster radioed for help. "We have encountered an IED and small arms fire," the colonel reported. "We need medical help and air support."

Soon two Bradley Fighting Vehicles carrying additional soldiers came roaring down the road. The huge, heavily armored tank-like vehicles stopped and dropped their rear hatches.

The soldiers on the Bradleys rushed out and crouched alongside a wall to direct their fire at a farmhouse near the bomb crater. That was where the shooting was coming from.

Within minutes they had captured five insurgents. Then two Apache helicopters swooped down firing automatic weapons. The remaining insurgents fled.

Bradley Fighting Vehicles

The Bradley Fighting Vehicle is a large, tank-like vehicle. Its main role is to move troops, provide fire cover for soldiers during a battle, and defeat enemy tanks.

This heavily armored vehicle has several weapons. It has a chain gun, which can fire single shots or many bullets like a machine gun. The gun is powered by a motor that moves a chain through the weapon. As the chain moves, it loads and fires bullets, then ejects the used bullet cartridges all in one smooth motion. The Bradley also has an anti-tank missile launcher and two grenade launchers.

The helicopters landed and medical workers, called medics, rushed to the damaged Humvee. Sergeant Haycox helped the medics treat the wounded. Then, he helped them load the injured into the helicopter. They were flown to a nearby hospital. Some of the injured survived, but others did not.

Sergeant Joshua Haycox knew he would never forget that day. He would also never forget the fact that it very easily could have been him injured or killed in the Humvee explosion.

FACTFILE

Humvees as Ambulances

When the rear cargo area of a Humvee is set up to be used as an ambulance it can carry up to eight wounded soldiers. It usually also carries medical equipment such as oxygen and intravenous supplies (for IVs), as well as a full supply of first aid equipment, including bandages, antiseptic, and splints. At first the ambulance Humvee was the only Humvee with air conditioning. This was important in order to keep injured soldiers as comfortable and stable as possible. But now the newer up-armored Humvees all have air conditioning.

Chapter SIX

Who Drives a Humvee?

All branches of the U.S. armed forces use Humvees, but they are used mainly by the Army and Marines. Special training is required in order for a soldier to be approved to drive a Humvee.

Soldiers are trained in how to drive and maintain their vehicles. When the training is complete, a special Humvee driver's license is issued to the soldier, who is then authorized to drive the vehicle. Training usually lasts between five days and two weeks.

Humvees are very versatile. They can be used for many operations by being fitted with many types of equipment. Those trained to drive and maintain Humvees must be able to operate and take care of the vehicles in any of their forms.

Soldiers are trained by driving Humvees over different types of terrain. They drive off-road, over steep, bumpy dirt roads, and through rivers. They are also trained in how to drive into a battle area. They learn to maneuver when the Humvee is being used in combat (with a gunner on top), or how to speed to the rescue while driving an ambulance-version Humvee.

The U.S. Navy is not usually associated with operations on land, but Navy SEALs also use Humvees. SEALs are special operations troops highly

▼ Anyone who drives a Humvee must also know how to maintain it. This soldier checks her Humvee's oil.

FACTFILE

Training at Home

Lots of soldiers currently serving in Iraq drive Humvees. Many of them learned how to drive the large vehicles back home in the United States before they went overseas. There is a 550,000-acre training facility in northwest Florida where soldiers learn to drive Humvees. Steep hills, deep rivers, and rugged roads simulate the environment soldiers will encounter once they are in Iraq.

trained in approaching targets on land from the air and the water. (SEAL stands for SEa, Air, and Land.) These highly skilled sailors must also be trained in driving Humvees for land-based attacks. They need to be able to move into areas quickly and get out undetected. If they are detected, they need to be able to outdrive their opponents in order to get away.

Humvee drivers practice driving cross-country in large convoys. In this case, drivers must learn to protect the convoy, while keeping all the vehicles together. This includes blocking intersections in city streets so that convoys can roll through safely.

To simulate combat situations, instructors shoot at student-driven Humvees with a paintball gun. Sometimes instructors yell in the ears of students to shake them up, simulating the noise and chaos of a combat situation. Instructors will also fire weapons from inside the Humvee so that drivers can get used to the sound of returning fire being sent out by their fellow soldiers in the Humvee. These simulated combat situations help get soldiers ready for the difficult duty they will face when they drive Humvees in real combat situations.

Soldiers who drive Humvees while in the military are well prepared for many jobs outside the armed forces. This includes truck, bus, fire engine, or ambulance drivers. Their Humvee training and experience make them able to handle the special pressures that such drivers face every day. For

▼ Some Humvee trainees use simulators, which imitate real conditions on the battlefield. This soldier is practicing with a mock machine gun on top of a simulated Humvee.

example, those who choose to become ambulance drivers must often be able to drive their vehicles through busy city streets while still obeying traffic laws. They must balance the safety of other vehicles on the road and of pedestrians with the urgency of the medical condition of the patient they are carrying.

Since soldiers who drive Humvees have experience in high-pressure situations, some decide to become Emergency Medical Service (EMS)

FACTFILE

Disaster Training

Humvees are not only useful, versatile vehicles for combat situations. They also work well during disaster relief. Natural disasters such as hurricanes or tornadoes disrupt or destroy people's lives and homes. They can even destroy entire cities.

Those trained in driving Humvees can race to the rescue in these situations, confident in their vehicle's ability to drive through rough or damaged terrain. That is why the American Red Cross offers its volunteers training on Humvees.

▲ Former Humvee drivers have succeeded as Emergency Medical Service (EMS) technicians. They already know how to work in high-stress situations.

technicians after they leave the military. These workers are often the first on the scene of an accident. They must determine the condition of any people hurt in the accident and do what is necessary to prepare them for their trip to the hospital. Then the EMS technician works with the ambulance driver to get the person to the nearest hospital as quickly as possible.

No matter what career a Humvee driver chooses after serving in the military, there is no doubt that the valuable training and experience gained behind the wheel of this multi-purpose vehicle will help prepare the soldier for anything he or she decides to do.

camouflage—Characteristics, such as color and shape, that help something blend in with its surroundings.

chassis—The body of a vehicle.

convoy—A group of vehicles traveling together.

grenade—A small explosive device that is thrown by hand or launched at its target.

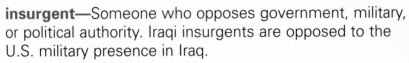

gunner—A soldier who is stationed at the top of a Humvee and who operates the gun mounted on the turret.

insurgent—Someone who opposes government, military, or political authority. Iraqi insurgents are opposed to the U.S. military presence in Iraq.

mine—An explosive device usually buried in the ground.

missile—An explosive device which is fired at a target on the ground or in the air.

munitions—Weapons and ammunition.

night vision viewer—A device which allows people to see in the dark by collecting and boosting the small amounts of light that are available at night.

PSYOPS—"Psychological operations" used to keep the opposing side nervous and uneasy.

riding shotgun—Riding in the seat next to the driver.

runflat tires—Tires which can work even after they are punctured.

surveillance—Watching in secret, spying.

transmission—The part of a motor vehicle that sends power made by the engine to the wheels, enabling the vehicle to move.

turret—An armored revolving tower in which a gun and gunner can be stationed on a tank or Humvee.

Books

Green, Michael, and Greg Stewart. *Humvee at War.* Osceola, Wis.: Zenith Press, 2005.

Healy, Nick. *High Mobility Vehicles: The Humvees.* Mankato, Minn.: Capstone Press, 2005.

Munro, Bill. *Humvee.* Wiltshire, U.K.: Crowood Press, 2003.

Zaloga, Steven. *HMMWV Humvee 1980–2005: US Army Tactical Vehicle.* Oxford, U.K.: Osprey, 2006.

Internet Addresses

http://www.amgeneral.com/vehicles_hmmwv.php/
  AM General is the company that created and built the Humvee. This page includes pictures and information about Humvees.

http://www.army.mil/fact_files_site/hmmwv
  Army Fact File with information about Humvees.

http://www.globalsecurity.org/military/systems/ground/m998.htm
  Information about many types of Humvees, including ambulances and up-armored Humvees.

INDEX